JESUS, I WANT TO TALK WITH YOU

Edward Carter, SJ

JESUS, I WANT TO TALK WITH YOU

CONTEMPORARY PRAYERS

ALBA BOOKS

CANFIELD, OHIO 44406

Imprimi Potest:

    Robert F. Harvanek, S.J.
    Provincial
    Chicago Province, Society of Jesus
    September 1, 1972

Nihil Obstat:

    Edward B. Brueggeman, S.J.
    Censor Deputatus

Imprimatur:

    August J. Kramer
    Administrator of the Archdiocese of Cincinnati
    September 20, 1972

Library of Congress Catalog Card Number 73 - 75617
ISBN 0 - 8189 - 1142 - 5

The author acknowledges the use of the following copyrighted material
Excerpts from **The New American Bible** (c) 1970 used herein by per-
mission of the Confraternity of Christian Doctrine, copyright owner.

PREFACE

Our relationship with Jesus is meant to touch everything about our existence. Whether we work, or play, or love one another, or feel joy, or pain—all these and other aspects of our daily living we know are of interest to Jesus. He wants us to talk to Him about them. This book of prayers, then, covers all sorts of human experiences.

The following prayers are based upon life as I, and people I know, and you, too, have experienced it. Many of the prayers also contain passages from Scripture. I have tried not to use these in a forced manner, but in a relevant way to show how the word of God has constant application to our daily existence. Two main channels through which God speaks to us are Scripture and the events out of which our daily lives are shaped. We are meant to blend the two together.

Because prayer should come out of the experience of our daily lives, I believe the language of prayer in general should be ordinary, sometimes profoundly ordinary in its everydayness. I believe the language of prayer should also be direct and familiar, and that we should talk to Jesus as to someone who is very close to us. I believe it should have a simplicity about it, but a penetrating simplicity which gets at the heart of human experiences. These, then, are characteristics which I have tried to blend into the style which is found in the following prayers.

This book of prayers is an attempt to unite prayer with life and life with prayer. It is an attempt to help us pray always as Saint Paul bids us: "Rejoice always, never cease praying...." (1 Thes 5:16-17).

I wish to thank in a very special way Sister Joan Guntzelman, S.C. for her careful typing of the manuscript and for her other valuable assistance. Gratitude is also due to Father Edward Brueggeman, S.J. and Father Carl Moell, S.J. for their suggestions.

Edward Carter, S.J.

CONTENTS

Jesus, I Want to Talk with You

● Jesus, I want to talk with you. I want to talk with you about myself, and other people, and all sorts of happenings.

● Lord, I want to talk with you about the people in my life, about my work and play, about my joys and sufferings. I want to talk with you about others, too—those I know, and those unknown to me. I want to ask you for help, for strength, for encouragement, for enlightenment. I want to ask for your love. I want to ask you to bless others, too.

● Jesus, you are my God. You are also my brother. You are my friend, too. As I pray to you, you want me to feel free to discuss anything with you. You're interested in everything that's a part of my life. You're always ready to listen. In your love and concern for me, you're always inviting me to come closer to you, and speak.

● Jesus, I want to talk with you.

We Need Each Other

● We can pretend we don't need one another, Lord. But that won't change the way you've really made us.

● You didn't make us isolated individuals, individuals with no need to share with the other, to be with the other, to give to the other, to receive from the other.

● Lord, instead you made us as people who are to walk life's road hand in hand. To walk alone, then, Jesus, is a man's own folly, his unwise decision. It is his refusal to be what you want him to be—a social being.

● We need one another—so that we can weep together, anguish together, rejoice together, be happy together, work together, play together.

● Lord, let us see all this. Let us see how much we need one another. Don't let pride blind us. Don't let us think we are self-sufficient, needing nobody but ourselves. Jesus, help us to remember that no one is meant to be an island—an isolated piece of humanity.

Lord, She'll Never Walk Again

● She was driving too fast, Jesus. The curve appeared too suddenly. There was the slam of brakes, and a frightening screech of sliding tires. There was her last-second, frantic struggle for control. Then the awful crash. And, finally, deadening silence.

● The ambulance got her to the hospital alive—but permanently paralyzed.

● Lord, before the crash she had what so many admire. She had physical beauty, artistic talent, money, and social position.

● Jesus, she has traumatically learned how fleeting such things can be:

> And there was great mourning for
> Israel, in every place where they
> dwelt,
> and the rulers and the elders
> groaned.
> Virgins and young men languished,
> and the beauty of the women was
> disfigured. (1 Mc 1:25-26)

● The shock of how quickly her life had changed was overwhelming, Jesus. She was near despair. So suddenly, so much of what her life had rested on was now stripped away. She was thrown back on inner self, her inner resources. And it was a strange new life.

● Help her, Jesus. She needs you badly.

It's a Beautiful Day, Jesus

● It's a great day, Jesus, a beautiful day, and in more ways than one.

● Outside it's beautiful, Jesus. The air is crisp, shot through with October freshness. The leaves fascinate me with their colors, with their golds, and reds, and browns. The sky is clear blue, deep blue, all blue. The sun is autumn bright.

● It's a beautiful day inside, too, Jesus—inside me. I feel all aglow today, especially glad to be alive. Life, with its beautiy, its grandeur, its expansiveness, its possibilities for greatness, lays hold of me, deeply attracts me.

● On a day like this, Jesus, I feel spurred on to be what I am supposed to be, to be what you want me to be. I feel especially inspired to love, to love you, to love my fellowmen.

● Thanks, Jesus, for today.

Simple Experiences

●   Lord, sometimes I think we become too complex, too sophisticated. We can miss so much of the joy and contentment wrapped up in simple experiences.

●   The warm, receptive smile of a friend—isn't this more precious than a lot of other things? Like, I mean, a lot of things which cost a lot of money?

●   And to be able to see a sunset, or feel the snow flakes falling, or smell the freshness of a rose—are we interested enough in these experiences, Lord?

●   To give a lot of attention to big, noisy parties, and to pass over the beauty of simple meals taken with loved ones, does this make sense, Lord?

●   Or to work just for the paycheck, and to count as nothing the sense of service and accomplishment in a job well done—this is kind of crazy, isn't it, Lord?

●   Jesus, what makes us too often miss the real experience?

A Little Girl Was Raped, Lord

● She's only eleven. She was walking down the street alone on her way to school. A car pulled up. The man forced her in and drove to a wooded area.

● He did his thing, Lord. And what a mean and vicious thing. He raped her, as she lay innocent, helpless, frightened.

● What an ugly show of man's sinfulness, Lord.

● Something like this hits us right between the eyes, Jesus. It reminds us that there's a seething, loathsome side of the human condition. It makes us weep that things are so. Make it inspire us, too, Jesus, to try to make things better.

● Take care of the little girl, Lord. Her first experience of sex, a beautiful gift, was so ugly, traumatic, soul-shattering. Hold her, Lord, and make her feel secure. Help the man, too, Lord. Help him to be sorry. Forgive him, Lord.

Jesus, We're Supposed To Be Joyful and Happy

● There's a lot of pain, and suffering, and evil in life, Lord. The human situation never lets us forget all this. But, still, life is meant to be joyful—basically joyful and happy.

● We Christians should especially be happy. If we're not, Lord, it seems like we're betraying your Good News.

● Sometimes we go about living as if we didn't believe in you, as if you had not become man, as if you didn't come to give us the fulness of life, as if you had not risen.

● You, and the Father, and the Holy Spirit love us mightily, Jesus—this is our happiness.

● Being able to love God in return—this is our happiness, too.

● Loving one another, working together, playing together, just being together—this is our happiness.

● Marveling at God's sunset, at his mountains and waters, and trees, and meadows—this is our happiness.

● We have all sorts of reasons to be happy, Lord. Really, to be a Christian should mean to be happy: "Rejoice in the Lord always! I say it again. Rejoice!" (Phil 4:4).

●

A Hospital

● Lord, as I walk down the corridors of the hospital, I think of all the different kinds of people, attitudes, and happenings within these walls.

● New life, in its awful mystery, is joining us. What lies ahead of these new-born babies, Lord? Which of them will answer the challenge of life, and become beautiful persons? Which will go astray, and wallow in sinfulness?

● Some here are dying, Jesus. What are they thinking about? Do some of them feel they have wasted their lives, wasted precious opportunities to be what you wanted them to be? Are there others who look back on a life well-lived, and who think that, despite the pain and the suffering at times, it was all so worth it?

● Lord, are there those here who are bitter in their illness, and others who are growing through their sufferings?

● And the doctors and nurses and others who work here, Lord, what are their attitudes? How many look upon their jobs as precious opportunities to serve you in the sick and the injured? How many have developed an impersonal, almost mechanical, attitude toward the patients?

● Jesus, help all the people in this hospital according to their needs.

Adult Books, Magazines, and Movies

● Those pornographic shops keep multiplying, Lord. One of their big come-ons is to have signs plastered all over the front windows which read, "Adults Only." A friend of mine has a pretty good comeback. He says those signs should rather read, "Adolescents Only."

● The point he's making is that the so-called adults who frequent these places are really acting in an adolescent or childish manner. They're betraying their adult maturity by wasting their time on a lot of trash. They're aiming their sexuality in the wrong direction.

● Nobody is perfectly mature, is he, Lord? If we're sexually mature, this doesn't mean we don't have other signs of immaturity. We're immature when we don't act as we should, when we aim some God-given talent or capacity at a wrong object, in the wrong direction. Then, in our own way, we're acting like the people going after pornography—we're looking for fulfillment in the wrong way.

● Help us to grow in Christian maturity, Jesus. Part of this growing is realizing there's pain involved. One of the big reasons we remain kind of stunted is that we're afraid of this pain. Help us, Lord, to conquer this fear of suffering. Help us to grow into that fulness you intend for us: "I came that they might have life and have it to the full" (Jn 10:10).

Only Today Is Fully Mine, Jesus

● Jesus, only today is fully mine. Yesterday is past. I cannot reclaim it, and live it again. Tomorrow I cannot yet say is mine, or even that it will certainly be. One day of my life, whenever that may be, will have no tomorrow.

● Lord, I know that at times I live too much in the past, or dream too often of the future. I can learn from the past and be buoyed up by the future, but neither should control the focus of my attention.

● Lord, be with me today. Help me see how wonderful today is, with its myriad possibilities for life, and love, and accomplishment. Let me see the grandeur which is now, rather than be distracted by the inflated memories of times past, or the unrealistic musings of what might only some day be.

● Lord, give me the courage to face the difficult aspect of today. Don't allow me to flee the pain I'm supposed to endure this hour, however slight it may be, and yet boast that some tomorrow I will heroically bear great trials and tribulations.

● Lord, keep me honest with myself just for today— and then tomorrow I'll ask your help again. Let me always remember what you've told us, Jesus: "Enough, then, of worrying about tomorrow. Let tomorrow take care of itself" (Mt 6:34).

He Was a White Boy Looking at a Black Boy, Lord, But He Didn't See Black

● I'll never forget the story, Lord. A black man was talking to a white audience about the race problem. His brief story probably said more than a twenty page speech on theory could have.

● His little son was the only black in the class. One day he got into a fight with one of the white boys. The white boy went to the teacher and said, "He hit me." The teacher asked, "Which one?" The white boy pointed to the little black boy and said, "The one with the glasses."

● Lord, the wisdom of babes can often unmask the adult, lay him bare to the truth, shatter his facade. The little white boy was not yet color conscious, race conscious. He was mad at the black boy, but when he pointed him out, he didn't see black. He saw another boy like himself, another human being.

● Lord, you speak to us sometimes through the words and attitudes and actions of little ones. The question is, are we too sophisticated, too prejudiced, too worldly-wise to listen? There's a lot in what you said, Jesus: "I assure you, unless you change and become like little children, you will not enter the kingdom of God. Whoever makes himself lowly, becoming like this child, is of greatest importance in that heavenly reign" (Mt 18:3-4).

She's Been Rejected in Love, Lord

● She's only eighteen. But life seems over already. She doesn't feel like eating. She doesn't feel like doing anything. She doesn't even feel like living.

● She says she loved him an awful lot, Jesus. She says it was her first real love. She says she could feel it coming. He started acting kind of different, kind of cold. Then one day he told her.

● She's hurt, Jesus, hurt real bad. She's been rejected, and she's crushed, bruised real bad, bruised where it heals so slowly, in the depths of the heart.

● Help her, Jesus. Lift her up tenderly. Show her that she's good, and worthwhile, with all sorts of possibilities waiting for her. Show her that her life isn't over, but just sort of beginning. Help her, Jesus.

Jesus, Sometimes You've Got Other Ideas

● Lord, I can wake up in the morning, having things pretty well mapped out for the day. I've got things lined up as to how I'm going to serve you.

● But, Jesus, sometimes you have different ideas. Sometimes your thoughts are not my thoughts. Sometimes what you want of me on a particular day is pretty much of a surprise to me.

● Unexpected things can happen—like two or three people asking me for time I had planned for something else. One may have a problem which is particularly annoying this day. It helps just to talk about it, although there may be no immediate solution. Another may just want a kind of extended rapport with another human—to share a sorrow, or a joy, or to lessen a feeling of loneliness.

● Lord, help me realize all the different ways you can speak to me—like through the needs of others. Let me be flexible enough, concerned enough, open enough, to change my schedule—today, or any day.

She Isn't Very Pretty, Jesus

● The boys don't look at her too often—or too long. Her looks aren't that much. She does her part. She's neat, and clean. Her hair is nicely fixed. But she doesn't have much to work with, Jesus.

● Lord, don't allow her to sour on life. Life won't be easy for her. But she's still got a lot to give the world. She's kind, and good, and she wants to help people. Let her see these gifts she has, Lord. Don't let her be discouraged, crushed by that fake mystique that says looks are everything—especially for a woman.

● I think you have a special place in your heart for people like her, Jesus. She has to fight a little harder to keep back her tears. She has a harder time telling herself that she does matter, that she is worthwhile. Let her know, Jesus, how much you love her, how much she means to you:

> Can a mother forget her infant,
>   be without tenderness for the child
>   of her womb?
> Even should she forget,
>   I will never forget you.

(Is 49:15)

A Wedding

●   Sue looked pretty with her striking blond hair, her ever-ready smile, and her flowing gown. As always, she was gracious and kind to everybody. Ray looked handsome. He was, of course, at least a little nervous. Otherwise, he was the same—so friendly, so approachable. It was a great day for Sue and Ray, Lord. It was their wedding day. I love them both. I was glad for them. I was glad I was there.

●   Each wedding is so different, isn't it Lord? That's because each couple is unique. The bride and groom, each unique, join together. We have something wonderfully new and beautiful and mysterious. In one sense, bride and groom remain the same. But, also, how different they become. They've pledged to share one another's uniqueness, deep down, to the core of their beings: "That is why a man leaves his father and mother and clings to his wife, and the two of them become one body" (Gn 2:24).

●   Sue and Ray will be happy, Jesus. I know they'll be. They're made of the stuff which creates happiness. They're loving, and selfless, and kind, aware of the other.

●   They'll know good times and bad times. They'll have many moments of simple contentment. They'll know rarer times of deepest happiness. They'll have their problems, too, and times of pain, and perhaps moments of anguished suffering. But through it all, they'll be together—loving each other.

● Bless this marriage by being with them, Lord, just as you blessed through your presence a wedding long ago. "On the third day there was a wedding at Cana in Galilee, and the mother of Jesus was there. Jesus and his disciples had likewise been invited to the celebration" (Jn 2:1-2).

Jesus, We Should Want To Be the Best

● Lord, whatever may be our task in life, we should have a desire to excel.

● We shouldn't want this, Jesus, from a motive of selfish pride. We shouldn't want to excel so that we can have the spot-light focused on us as we strut arrogantly across life's stage. We should want to excel at our tasks because of you, and because of the brothers you want us to serve.

● Whether a person is a nurse, or a carpenter, or a housewife, or a doctor, or a store clerk, or a teacher, or whatever, he or she should give his best, Lord. Not to give one's best is to compromise the dignity of work, and the responsibility of talent, and the opportunity to serve you and mankind.

● To strive to excel at our task, Lord, does not mean developing ulcers and other signs of nervous tension. You don't want this. To excel means to give our reasonable best in a human way. To excel means that amid the sweat of honest effort there is a sense of being at peace with ourselves. To excel means there is a satisfaction in knowing that we are doing what you want us to do, in the way you want.

● Jesus, help us to give our best according to your will.

He Took an Overdose of Heroin

● His picture was in a news magazine. There he was, sprawled out on the steps. He was kind of young looking. But he won't get any older. He was dead.

● He had taken an overdose of heroin. How long had he been on the stuff, Lord? Did he get hooked because his buddy dared him to take some? Was he trying to escape from pain and anguish? Or had he just been kind of bored with life and wanted a high?

● Whatever the reason, he's now dead. He was made in your image, Lord:

> God created man in his image;
>   in the divine image he created him....
> (Gn 1:27)

Like all of us he was created for a high purpose. What went wrong, Lord? Why did his life come to such a warped end?

● This drug problem makes me sad, Lord. It's hitting the young more and more. Fresh, beautiful lives are being suddenly twisted, dehumanized, crushed out. I want to help, but I don't know exactly what to do. What should I be doing, Jesus?

Lord, Your Love Is Now

● Jesus, sometimes I'm too forgetful of how much you love me.

● Your love is now, not relegated to the past, not promised only for the future. Your love is constantly with me in all its depth, and beauty, and tenderness, and strength.

● Your love is now in the sense of being loved by another, in the simple joys of everyday, in the sense of accomplishment, in the thrill at nature's beauty, in the feeling that life is beautiful despite its pain. All these are gifts of your love.

● Your love is now, Jesus, as it supports me when I experience failure or pain, when I feel rejected, unloved, and lonely.

● Jesus, your love is now in what it wants of me each day, every day. Your love is now as you ask my help—my help in the making of a better world, a world in which there will be less hatred and more love, less war and more peace, less destitution and more equal distribution of goods, less selfishness and more selflessness, less rejection of God and more love and acceptance of Him.

● Lord, help me always to realize that your love is now, in every now, in so many different ways:

Yes, God so loved the world
that he gave his only Son,
that whoever believes in him may not die
but may have eternal life.

(Jn 3:16)

They're Happily Married, Lord

● Lord, she told me she loves him just like she did on their wedding day. By this she doesn't mean her love hasn't grown, but that it's remained fresh, vital, alive.

● They're a testimony to the multi-splendored greatness of married love—a testimony to what it can achieve if allowed to unfold its gifts, if allowed to work its quiet transformation. They're a testimony to married love's beauty, tenderness, concern, selflessness, creativity.

● They've borne precious children together. They've worked hard together, they've danced. They've laughed and they've cried. They've prayed together, simply but so beautifully, and welcomed you into their love.

● They say it's been great, this life together. They've believed in love, what it can do, its power for good in so many ways, and their trust has been repaid.

● Thanks, Lord, for making them such beautiful people. Thanks for their happy marriage.

I Feel Depressed, Lord

● I'm feeling kind of low, Jesus. Things aren't going so well. I get depressed occasionally just like other people, and, I guess, for the same reasons.

● Sometimes I feel people don't understand me. Sometimes, despite my best efforts, it seems all I hear is what I'm doing wrong. Sometimes I make a big effort at loving others, and I don't feel loved in return—not that I should stop loving because of this. At other times it's my work—I keep at it, but I don't seem to be accomplishing much.

● Lord, when I'm feeling low I should fight against it. It helps if I remind myself that I still mean a lot to you. I believe that you love me, and deeply, and everlastingly. What I have to do is not let go of your love: "Who will separate us from the love of Christ? Trial, or distress, or persecution, or hunger, or nakedness, or danger, or the sword? . . . Yet in all this we are more than conquerors because of him who has loved us" (Rom 8:35-37).

● You have given each of us a mission, a role to fulfill, Lord. I can't call upon a substitute to accomplish that task. This is a great privilege—and a great responsibility. When I get depressed, help me to remember all this, Jesus. Help me rise above the depression. Help me get on with my purpose in life.

She Had Sex, Lord

● It was her first time, Lord. She had always said she would wait until marriage. But things kept building up more and more. I guess they were seeing too much of one another. When it happened, nothing else seemed to matter.

● She's pregnant, Lord. And he's not the same toward her. She says it's funny—she said she did it because she loved him. Now he's turned cool, says he's not sure he really loves her.

● She's confused, Lord. She says she's not sure just what love is, and what sex is. Help her, Jesus.

Superficial Living

● Lord, it's kind of easy to glide along, barely cutting the surface of life, of the really real.

● We have a tendency, Jesus, to refuse to live—I mean to live down deep at the heart of life.

● Why are we like this, Jesus? Are we too lazy to take the effort to live deeply? Are we satisfied with less happiness because deep happiness just costs too much?

● Jesus, are we superficial in our experiences of life because we don't take enough time to reflect on the meaning of life, how it should be lived, how to experience the really real?

● Jesus, help us ask the right questions so that we can better avoid superficial living. Help us also find the right answers.

Jim Died Today

● He was a seminarian. He wanted to be a priest, but he never will. He died this morning. It was only about a week after his third cancer operation. Complications set in—the doctors think a blood clot killed him. He was only twenty-four.

● I lived on the same floor with Jim. He was a real man. He never complained of his illness. He never said, "Why me, Lord?" I'll ask the question for him, Jesus. Why did he have cancer? Why did you take him at such an early age? Why did his life end so prematurely, a life which held such promise, a life which wanted to do so much, a life which will be so deeply missed by those who knew and loved him?

● You've been asked these questions so many times before, Jesus. God's ways are not always our ways, nor are his thoughts always our thoughts:

> And scarce do we guess the things on
>   earth,
>   and what is within our grasp we
>   find with difficulty;
>   but when things are in heaven, who
>   can search them out?

(Wis 9:16)

● I feel sad, Jesus, that Jim has left us. I wish now I had stopped in a few more times to say hello. I'll miss him. We all will. Thanks, Jesus, for keeping him with us as long as you did.

Jesus, There Are Things I Want

● I want to give myself to your love, Lord, not fear it, not reject it, not think that I am happier without it. I want to love you, Lord, in all sorts of ways, in everything I do. These are big words, I know, Jesus, and too often I forget them. But I really do want to live by them.

● I want to love the human family—my brothers and my sisters. Some I want to love in a real special way. And I want to be loved, too. I want to work and to accomplish and to be useful to others. I want to rejoice with others, and make their joy my own. And their sorrow—I want to be big enough to share this, too. I want them to share my joy and sorrow, too, Lord.

● I want to laugh, and play, and see the funny side of things. I want to see baseball games and football games; I want to listen to music. I want to walk by the seashore, and just relax. I want to taste the freshness of spring, and feel the cold of winter's snow: "The fact is that whether you eat or drink—whatever you do—you should do all for the glory of God" (1 Cor 10:31).

● I want to suffer as I should, and rejoice as I should. I want to be optimistic, not pessimistic. I want to be quick to praise, slow to condemn.

● These are some of the things I want, Jesus. You want them for me, too, Lord. Help me, Lord.

I Was Hurting, Lord

● I was really hurting, Lord, deep down. It was a pain of the spirit, but so real and overwhelming that I was tempted to trade it off for a real big physical suffering.

● Thanks, Jesus, for helping me. All of a sudden I felt you with me in a special way. Then I could work myself out of it.

● Let me always come to you when I'm hurting, Lord— not only then, but certainly then also. I know you'll help me in some way. You'll give me some sort of answer, some sort of relief: "Ask, and you will receive. Seek, and you will find. Knock, and it will be opened to you. For the one who asks, receives. The one who seeks, finds. The one who knocks, enters" (Mt. 7:7-8).

Jesus, I Want You

● Jesus, I want to be close to you. I want to feel united to you, one with you. Lord, the Psalmist has words for me:

> O God, you are my God whom I
>   seek;
>   for you my flesh pines and my soul
>   thirsts....

(Ps 63:2)

● Jesus, you give meaning to my life, you gather up the pieces. You show me how it all fits together—the work and the play, the joy and the pain, the laughter and the tears.

● The closer I am to you, Jesus, the more meaning I see in life. Without you I am helpless. I am adrift, I am lost.

● Take me closer, Jesus, make my life more yours. Make me more yours, make me more one with you.

My Brothers Are Crying Out to Me, Jesus

● Jesus, the cries of my brothers are getting to me. I feel guilty, plagued by the thought that I should be doing more for them. Their hunger, their nakedness, their sickness, their despair—all that is shouting out loud and clear.

● Their cries ring in my ears, reverberate round and round, refuse to die out. The cries come from all around the world.

● Lord, the stories of their miseries seem without end. But just one of them is too much—like the story of the black family and their rat-infested dwelling. The rats started eating away at the little children as they slept. So the adults had to take their turns at the night-watch.

● Lord, why should this have to be? Why should people made in your image and likeness have to sleep in a rat house, be without clothes, be without food?

● I feel I should give more of what I have to my poorer and less fortunate brothers, Jesus. I feel I should help them more in other ways, too. Lord, your words bother me: "I was hungry and you gave me no food, I was thirsty and you gave me no drink. I was away from home and you gave me no welcome, naked and you gave me no clothing. I was ill and in prison and you did not come to comfort me" (Mt 25:42-43).

I Should Be Thankful, Lord

● Jesus, too often I take your gifts for granted. I'm not nearly thankful enough. I'm like the nine lepers you cured who failed to thank you! "One of them, realizing that he had been cured, came back praising God in a loud voice. He threw himself on his face at the feet of Jesus and spoke his praises. This man was a Samaritan. Jesus took the occasion to say, 'Were not all ten made whole? Where are the other nine? Was there no one to return and give thanks to God except this foreigner?'" (Lk 17:15-18).

● You've given me a healthy body, Lord. There are thousands who can't see, or can't walk, or can't hear. Don't let me take good health for granted, Jesus. Thank you.

● You've given me my Christian faith, Lord. While millions walk without your light to guide them, I have been given your truth. Thank you, Lord.

● Thank you, Jesus, for becoming man. Thank you for all the ways in which you give yourself to me.

● Thank you for the sun, and the rain, and the snow, for peaked mountains and rolling meadows.

● Thank you, Jesus, for life itself, for the opportunity to love you and my fellow men.

● Thank you, Jesus, for the people in my life, the people who love me, who care for me, the people I love, the people I care for.

He Thinks He May Love Her Too Much, Lord

● His wife is seriously sick. She may die. He loves her mightily, and he wonders how he can live without her. Lord, he said something kind of strange. He said he wonders whether one person should love another so much.

● He was trying to say that if it's possible to lose someone you love so much, and if life seems impossible without that loved one, well then, maybe it's not the thing to do to love so much.

● Lord, I think he's wrong. Maybe his grief is clouding his thinking. I don't think it's possible to love a person too much—if it's really love, if it's really guided by your will.

● Lord, you made us for love. We're made to love God and to love human persons. If we have to watch out not to love another too much, then it seems we would be limiting our possibilities for growth, for life.

● Jesus, help the man to see that it's never the wrong thing to love another mightily. If it's really love, one guided by you, it's meant to grow, and grow, and grow. There may be deep pain involved, whether through a loss in death, or otherwise. But deep suffering is sometimes the price of deep love. You showed us this, didn't you, Jesus?

There's a Time for Everything, Jesus

● Lord, nature has a time for everything. There is the time of spring freshness—the time of blooming flowers, of budding trees, of greening grass. There is the time of the summer sun and the summer rain. There is the time of autumn crispness, of autumn leaves in red and gold and brown. There is the time of soft winter snow—glistening, white, and smooth.

● Jesus, we, too, have our cycle, a cycle of human experiences. There is a time for laughing and a time for weeping; a time for working and a time for playing; a time to speak and a time to keep silent; a time for joy and a time for sorrow; a time to be together and a time to be separated; a time to console and a time to be consoled; a time to help others and a time to be helped by them; a time for comprehending and a time for the pain of unknowing.

● Jesus, help us to realize that there's a time for everything. Help us to give ourselves to the right experience, in the right way, at the right time:

> There is an appointed time for
> everything,
>   and a time for every affair under
>   the heavens.

(Eccl 3:1)

I Went to a Funeral Yesterday, Jesus

● Yesterday I went to a funeral. I hadn't known Jack too well myself. I know Tom, his son, and Carol, his daughter-in-law. But the few times I had met Jack I was really impressed.

● People who knew him well say he was a great Christian. He was a kind man, a gentle man. He cared about his friends, but he cared about strangers, too. He must have been a great man, Jesus—the tears of his family tell me this. Despite their deep faith, they're grief-stricken at his sudden death—because they loved him so much.

● You wept, too, Jesus, over the death of your friend, Lazarus: "When Jesus saw her weeping, and the Jews who had accompanied her also weeping, he was troubled in spirit, moved by the deepest emotions. 'Where have you laid him?' he asked. 'Lord, come and see,' they said. Jesus began to weep, which caused the Jews to remark, 'See how much he loved him!'" (Jn 11:33-36).

● Lord, it's good for us to attend a funeral. A funeral brings home so vividly what life is all about. I need this reminder. Sometimes I go about living as if life on this earth will never end. Thanks for yesterday, Lord. Thanks for letting me be at the funeral—and please comfort Jack's family.

Love Takes a Lot of Work

● Lord, there's a contemporary poster which says that love is a lot of work. It's a very short saying, but it contains an awful lot of truth.

● Jesus, the failures of love number into the millions. I think a common cause for these failures is that a lot of people don't want to pay the price of love. Love is a glowing word, filled with charm and universal appeal. But beneath the surface of this four letter word lies a demand for constant selflessness, for sweat and tears, for the willingness to suffer immeasurably.

● Those who have succeeded in love know its price, Jesus. They have paid it, even when the demand was seemingly impossible. But they wouldn't have it any differently. They know, and have tasted, that to live is to love. They can appreciate, Lord, your summary of Christianity:

'You shall love the Lord your God
with your whole heart,
with your whole soul,
and with all your mind.'

This is the greatest and first
commandment. The second is like it:
'You shall love your neighbor as
yourself.'

(Mt 22:37-39)

He Was Drunk, Lord

● He was drunk. The only thing holding him up was the utility pole at the corner of the street. He was poorly dressed. Maybe his family was, too, if he got this way often. A working man's salary can't buy everything.

● There were a lot of other drunks on a lot of other streets that same day, Lord. I didn't see them. But they were there. Every day has its share. When we see a poor drunk, Lord, we may be looking at a lot more than just him. We may be looking at a wife beaten in a drunken rage. Or maybe we're looking at children, perhaps not beaten, but scarred in another way.

● Why can't we use your gifts properly, Lord—in a really human way? None of us is completely innocent. If we haven't misused drink, then it's something else. Show us, Jesus, how stupid we are in abusing your gifts. And please, Jesus, help the poor man I saw.

The Tenderness of Life

● Your manly tenderness attracts me, Jesus: "O Jerusalem, Jerusalem, murderess of prophets and stoner of those who were sent to you! How often have I yearned to gather your children, as a mother bird gathers her young under her wings, but you refused me" (Mt 23:37).

● Thank you for the tenderness of life, Jesus.

● Tenderness unites lovers, Jesus—the kiss and the touch and the look of tenderness.

● Tenderness makes the babe rest secure, Lord—a mother cuddles and hugs and looks in wonder at the child which is hers.

● Tenderness softens the harshness and the pain and the brutality of life. Lord, without touches of tenderness, who could endure death, and sickness, and loneliness, and emotional distress?

● Tenderness adds to the joys of life, Lord. It seems to make them more lasting, more human.

● Thanks, Jesus, for the tenderness of life.

Graduation Day

● It's another graduation day, Lord. It's another milestone in the lives of these students. It's a happy day!

● It's the end of something—the end of four years of college, years made up of all sorts of things. There's been enthusiasm and boredom, study and social life, close friendship and deep loneliness, times of bright hope and moments of near-despair.

● It's the beginning of something—the beginning of a new life, a life as scientist, or engineer, or salesman, or nurse, or teacher, or social worker, or ....

● Let it be a good beginning, Lord. Whatever their state of life, whatever their work or profession, let them be good at it. Let them go forth to make a better world. We need them, we need them a lot. As they go forth, let them be caught up with the vision of things as they ought to be:

> Then afterward I will pour out
>   my spirit upon all mankind.
> Your sons and daughters shall
>   prophesy,
>   your old men shall dream dreams,
>   your young men shall see visions ....

(Jl 3:1)

Your Blood Has Touched Black Men, Too, Jesus

● Your body was bruised, battered, smeared with blood. The cross dug down into your shoulder, dug deep down. You staggered and fell. You got up, and continued on.

● Then they nailed you to the cross, Jesus, and raised you up. Every nerve cried out, every muscle ached. You were burning with thirst, and the blood, blocked in its normal course, would suddenly burst forth with violent pain through your head, chest, and heart. And your spirit, Lord, it was weighed down with the deepest desolation, with an unbearable anguish.

● Jesus, why do some white Christians act as if you suffered all this for them, but not for the black man? Do they think your saving blood has touched them, but not the black man?

I'm Feeling Bored

● I'm just sitting here, Lord, doing nothing. I feel bored, listless, lethargic. I know I should work, but my whole being feels like a real heavy weight holding me back.

● All of us pass through these periods of boredom, Jesus. It's part of the human condition, one of the built-in pains of life. Only in eternity will we be fully alive, vibrant with a complete and dynamic and everlasting joyfulness.

> "Eye has not seen, ear has not heard,
>   nor has it so much as dawned on
>   man
>   what God has prepared for those
>   who love him."

(1 Cor 2:9)

● But if escape from all boredom is impossible, Lord, allow me to handle it properly. Don't let me surrender to it, indulge in it, cater to it, turn it into laziness. Don't let me neglect your work because of it.

● When I'm feeling bored, Lord, refresh me. Let me feel close to you, and touch me with your enthusiasm. Re-kindle my vision, and fire my will with the desire to be, to do, to act, to accomplish.

The Value of a Compliment

● Jesus, he told me I had done a good job. It's funny how a little thing like that can make a big difference. I feel refreshed. I feel like my work is worthwhile. I'm like a lot of other people. I don't mind hard work if I think it's doing some good. But I need someone to tell me this once in awhile.

● Jesus, you want us to help one another. Paying a person an honest compliment is one of the best ways.

● Why can't we affirm one another more often, Jesus? After all, that's only following your example. You constantly affirm us. You let us know that you love us, and appreciate our efforts to do your will.

● Jesus, do we hold back our compliments because we're afraid—afraid that in building up others we might become less ourselves? Help us see how silly this kind of thinking is, Lord.

● Help us, Lord, to encourage one another. Help us to be big enough to do this. Help us to do it sincerely, honestly, meaningfully.

We Don't Laugh Because We're Not Serious

● Jesus, we don't laugh enough because we're not serious enough.

● If we took you more seriously, we would be more light-hearted. If we received your message with utter seriousness, we would laugh more—at ourselves, at everything.

● To take your message seriously, Lord, to believe you very literally when you tell us and show us how much you love us—this would enable us to laugh more. Since you love us so much, what worry or anxiety can take away our peace and security and laughter—unless we allow it?

● You put it straight on the line, Jesus: "I warn you, then: do not worry about your livelihood, what you are to eat or drink or use for clothing. Is not life more than food? Is not the body more valuable than clothes? Look at the birds in the sky. They do not sow or reap, they gather nothing into barns; yet your heavenly Father feeds them. Are not you more important than they? Which of you by worrying can add a moment to his life-span?" (Mt 6:25-27).

She Looks Sad, Jesus

● She sits before me as I teach the class. Her face often looks very sad, Jesus. Why does she seem so sad? Does she feel unloved? Is there serious trouble in her family? Is she filled with some kind of despair?

● Are there many people burdened with a heavy sadness, Jesus? Are there many who surrender to sadness, whose taste for life has turned to bitterness?

● Hard and crushing as life may sometimes be, Jesus, you want us to conquer sadness. Scripture tells us:

> Do not give in to sadness,
>   torment not yourself with brooding;
> Gladness of heart is the very life of
>   man,
>   cheerfulness prolongs his days.

(Sir 30:21-22)

● Help us in moments of sadness, Jesus. Come close to us, touch us with your presence, put a smile on our faces. And, Jesus, help in a special way the girl in my class.

How Much Will I Still Have to Suffer, Lord?

● Jesus, you have left us these words: "Whoever wishes to be my follower must deny his very self, take up his cross each day, and follow in my steps. Whoever would save his life will lose it, and whoever loses his life for my sake will save it" (Lk 9:23-24).

● Each of us knows what you mean by those words, Jesus. To love is to suffer—and to love you is not exception to this rule.

● Sometimes I've suffered poorly, Jesus. I've complained and kind of wasted the suffering. Sometimes I've done better. Most of the time it's been a lot of little sufferings. Once in a while it's been a great big suffering which kind of split me apart. I felt like one big, open, raw nerve.

● How much suffering is still ahead of me, Jesus? But wait, I guess I'm asking the wrong question. I should ask, will I let you continue to show me the purpose of suffering? Will I let you convince me that suffering properly endured makes me a better person, one capable of greater love?

End of Another Day

● Another day is about over, Lord. As I grow older, the days and weeks and months seem to pass more quickly. Sometimes I feel the day slips away, eludes me, escapes me, before I even begin to exhaust its possibilities. I feel I've cheated you, and others, and myself. I feel I've lost opportunities to love, to be kind, to rejoice, to accomplish— to be what I should have been.

● Am I too much wasting my days, Lord? How can I improve the way I use them? I don't want to be just going through the motions. I don't want to go through my days robot-like. I want my days to be expressions of my innermost core, where I am most alive, where I am most sensitive to life's grandeur, where I am most myself.

● Jesus, allow me to meet each day with a new freshness, a creative freshness. Let me charge each day with a deepened faith, and hope, and love. Don't allow me to take even one day for granted. Each day is a precious gift to love God and man anew. This is your own attitude, Lord:

> We must do the deeds of him who
>   sent me
> while it is day.
> The night comes on
> when no one can work.

(Jn 9:4)

Allow Me To Learn and Grow, Lord

●   Lord, let me learn from life—in all sorts of ways.

●   Let me realize how much others have to teach me, if only I am open. Let me learn from their kindness, their concern for individuals, their joy, their courage, their patience in suffering, their dedication.

●   Lord, let me learn from my work. Let me profit from past mistakes, and become a better servant for others. Allow me to be humble in success, realizing that without you I am nothing.

●   Allow me to grow through personal relationships. Allow the pain and the joy and the beauty of these not to be wasted, but to take deep hold of my inner self, making me more what you desire that I be.

●   Allow everything to help me grow, Jesus—hard work and play, happiness and sorrow, simple things and grand experiences, the bitterness of life, and its sweetness, too. Allow me to grow in loving and being loved, in being accepted, in being misunderstood, in helping others, and in being helped by them. Allow me to learn, to grow, to profit from everything, Jesus. Life is precious, Jesus, and I don't want to waste it.

Troubles, Big and Small

●   Lord, the Psalmist prays:

> O Lord, hear my prayer,
> and let my cry come to you.
> Hide not your face from me
> in the day of my distress.
> Incline your ear to me;
> in the day when I call, answer me
> speedily.

(Ps 102:2-3)

●   Jesus, our troubles can be big or small. The little ones are with us almost daily. Some we experience in common, no matter what our walk of life. Others vary according to our vocation, and particular occupation. These little troubles constantly remind us that we are still pilgrims on the way. We have not yet come home. We have not yet achieved eternal life.

●   Occasionally, Lord, a trouble, a problem, a suffering, of the greatest proportions seems to overwhelm us. We feel crushed, helpless, almost near despair. Our pillows are tear-stained, and life seems joyless, its cup filled with bitter dregs.

●   In times of trouble, come near us, Lord, very near. Touch us tenderly. Let us feel your warmth, the glow of your love. If the trouble is to remain, let us bear with it as we should, Lord. Strengthen us, encourage us, comfort us, love us.

A Hundred Years — and Eternity

●   Lord, Scripture tells us:

The sum of a man's days is great
   if it reaches a hundred years:
Like a drop of sea water, like a grain
   of sand,
so are these few years among the
   days of eternity.

(Sir 18:7-8)

●   Jesus, some people live expecting no eternity. This life is an absolute for them. Death for them is the end, it is complete darkness, it is complete extinction, it is the beginning of complete nothingness.

●   Lord, I believe in eternity. Yet I have not always acted accordingly. Sometimes I have acted as if this present life were the only one. Sometimes I have acted no differently than the non-believer.

●   Lord, make me always aware of the reality of eternity. Let me see that a hundred years, a thousand years, a million years, are as nothing when compared to eternity.

●   Lord, let me realize that each day I am shaping my eternity. Let me realize also that I have the opportunity of helping others shape their eternity. Help me, Jesus. Help them, too, Jesus.

You Hung Upon a Tree

●   Jesus, you hung upon a tree. You hung there, rejected by so many of your beloved people, betrayed by Judas, denied by Peter, deserted by your disciples.

●   Jesus, you hung upon a tree. You seemed to be a tragic failure. But in reality you were a supreme success. You had accomplished your mission—a mission of love, of mercy, of kindness, of tenderness, of complete conformity to your Father's will.

●   Jesus, you hung upon a tree. You hung there in agony, an object of derision, smeared with your own blood, burning with fever, yet cold with the chill of approaching death, battered, bruised, exhausted, disfigured.

●   Jesus, you hung upon a tree, and you hung there for us. Never let us forget this:

> We had all gone astray like sheep,
>   each following his own way;
> But the Lord laid upon him
>   the guilt of us all.
>
> Though he was harshly treated, he
>   submitted
>   and opened not his mouth;
> Like a lamb led to the slaughter
>   or a sheep before the shearers,
>   he was silent and opened not his
>   mouth.

(Is 53:6-7)

Lord, He Said It Doesn't Cost a Dime To Be Nice

● Jesus, he said his father had told him it doesn't cost a dime to be nice to people. There's a lot in this saying for us to think about, Lord.

● During a life-time, there's all sorts of limitations which come our way, Lord. We can't always do what we want to do for you and others. Failures, and frustrations, and varying disabilities are part of the tapestry portraying the pictures of our lives.

● But, Lord, we can always be nice and kind to people. If we can control our selfishness and irritability, we can always offer the receptive smile, the kind word, the gentle touch.

● Perhaps, Lord, one of the biggest accomplishments of our lives is simply to be kind to people. Help us be this way, Jesus. Help us remember that it doesn't cost a dime.

I Was Feeling Sorry for Myself

● I was feeling sorry for myself, Jesus. Things weren't going well at all. I felt misunderstood, unappreciated, unjustly criticized.

● When this kind of feeling comes over me, Jesus, help me. Don't let me surrender to this mood, nourish it, wallow in it.

● Don't let me feel persecuted. Don't let me feel like one who is terribly abused. Let me see how small my sufferings are compared to those of a lot of people.

● When I start feeling sorry for myself, Jesus, remind me how much you put up with. Remind me that you didn't feel sorry for yourself. You just kept on doing what you were supposed to do. You were thankful for the opportunity to be about your Father's business.

They're Doing What They're Supposed To

● Joe told us the story, Jesus. He was driving along with his son, and he said, "I've often wondered why the trees and the flowers and the rocks are said to be praising God." His son answered, "Because they're doing what they're supposed to, Dad."

● The Psalmist tells us:

Praise the Lord from the earth,
    you sea monsters and all depths;
Fire and hail, snow and mist,
    storm winds that fulfill his word;
You mountains and all you hills,
    you fruit trees and all you cedars . . .

(Ps 148:7-9)

● Lord, non-rational creation praises you because it is accomplishing its purpose. It does what it is supposed to do. I praise you when I, too, do what I'm supposed to do. I don't always praise you—because sometimes I act contrary to your will. Jesus, help me to do better. Help me praise you more often.

People Are Lonely, Jesus

● He looks lonely, Lord. There he is on the TV screen, a stranger sitting alone in a bar, in a big city with millions of people—but he doesn't know any of them.

● A lot of aching human hearts, Lord, wish loneliness were just for people in TV plots. But that's not the way it is, Jesus. There are a lot of lonely people, real people. Some of them are so lonely that they feel split apart by it, and their whole existence feels like an open wound.

● Some are lonely because death has just taken one so deeply loved. They are shocked, dazed, numbed by their loneliness.

● Some are lonely because they feel no one really loves them, no one really cares.

● Some are lonely because they are far from home, far from loved ones.

● Some are lonely because they feel alienated from their inner core. They feel a stranger to themselves, with no distinct self-image, or one which is distinct, but which they hate.

● Some are lonely because life seems bizarre, crazy, ruthless.

● Loneliness hits us all, Jesus, at some time, for some reason. Help us, Jesus.

A Picnic

● It was a glorious and beautiful day for a picnic, Jesus. There was a blue sky, a clear sky, a June sky. The sun was invitingly warm, but not overly hot. And the cool breeze rustled through the variously shaped leaves. The grass was alive with greenness.

● It felt real good to be among friends, Lord, on such a day. We grown-ups enjoyed each other's company, but the children added a special something, too. Laura, Tommy, and Michael ran about, chasing butterflies, playing on the sturdy swings, and just bursting with energy in so many different ways.

● The food was simple, but very tasty. The grilled hamburgers, the potato chips, the cold drinks, the dessert—everything seemed just right.

● Thanks for the picnic, Lord. We need days like this to slow down the pace of life, and to help us remember that some of the greatest joys you give us are often the very simple ones.

Suffering

● Lord, you know what suffering is like. There was more than one moment of suffering in your life, but that night in Gethsemane must have been a special one: "Then Jesus went with them to a place called Gethsemani. He said to his disciples, 'Stay here while I go over there and pray.' He took along Peter and Zebedee's two sons, and began to experience sorrow and distress. Then he said to them, 'My heart is nearly broken with sorrow'" (Mt 26:36-38).

● We, too, Lord, experience suffering, and in so many different ways. There is that suffering, so unique, of seeing a loved one pass beyond the limits of space and time to eternal life. There is a rejoicing that the loved one has gone home, but, oh, there is a pain and a sense of sorrow, too—never again in this life to see that face, to hear that laugh, to listen to that voice, to touch that hand, to be at that side.

● There are other causes of suffering, too, Jesus. There is the lonely suffering of important decision-making—no one but ourselves can actually decide. There is the suffering of feeling misunderstood, of feeling unloved. Even when we experience love, there is the suffering of not being able to be united with the loved one as much as we desire.

● There are many other kinds of suffering, too, Lord. To mention a final example, there is the suffering of the loneliness of life itself. You have placed us within the mystery of life. Within the mystery of our free will we ultimately stand alone, choosing you, or rejecting you.

● Help us, Jesus, to bear life's suffering. Comfort us, strengthen us, draw us near to yourself, until finally you embrace us eternally, and all suffering, all tears, will be forever wiped away.

God Is My Hope

Lord, the Psalmist tells me:

Only in God is my soul at rest;
   from him comes my salvation.
He only is my rock and my
   salvation,
   my stronghold; I shall not be
   disturbed at all.

(Ps 62:2-3)

Lord, when darkness surrounds me, when the cross weighs heavily, when sadness comes, when life seems dreary, when my hope grows faint, let me remember those words of the Psalmist. Let me throw myself into your arms. Let me feel safe and secure, enlivened by your consoling strength.

Lord, in times of prosperity, let me also be conscious of my helplessness. Don't allow success in my work, praise from others, or the enjoyment of life to blind me to my need of you. Don't allow your gift which is the bright side of life to lessen my trust in you, my abandonment to you. Help me, Jesus.

There's So Much Violence, Lord

● Lord, where is all this violence leading to? Can the world so long endure the destructiveness of violence, its hatred, its divisiveness, its blatant brutalities, its disregard for human dignity?

● Will man ever be able to live in peace, Lord, without war and all its excruciating agony?

● Will darkened city streets ever be safe to walk again, Lord, without fear of muggings, of killings, of theft, of rape?

● Will the bombs continue to be placed in buildings, in airplanes, in automobiles? Will their victims continue to be blown into unrecognizable bits of human flesh?

● Will so many men continue to resort to violence because of quarrels, and labor disputes, and outright greed?

● Will T.V. and the movies continue to portray a morbid interest in inexcusable violence?

● Lord, prince of peace, let us taste your peace, let us rest in it. Let us be consumed with a desire to spread its message, however great the obstacles. It has been said that to light one candle is better than to curse the darkness. Lord, help me to be a candle-lighter.

Help Me To Be Patient, Jesus

● Lord, I don't always heed the words of Scripture concerning patience:

Accept whatever befalls you,
  in crushing misfortune be patient...

(Sir 2:4)

● There are times when I don't bear patiently with the faults of others. I feel annoyed that I should suffer because of their failings—forgetting that my faults could well be greater than theirs.

● I have been impatient with myself, and, perhaps, this has been a hidden type of pride.

● I have been impatient with the endless details of living, with the almost imperceptible results of my work for you, with the slowness with which some react to your word.

● Most of all, perhaps, I have been impatient when the cross was so heavy, when but a day of deep suffering seemed like an eternity, when I was so eager that the pain would quickly leave.

● Jesus, help me to realize the great importance of patience. Let me more clearly see that nothing worthwhile and longlasting is accomplished without it.

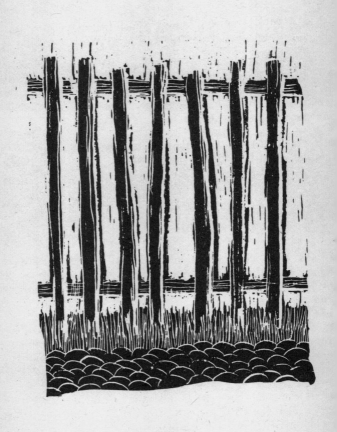

Simple and Unnoticed People

● Jesus, thanks for simple people. Thanks for those millions of people who are so unnoticed, but who form the heart of the human family.

● I've been privileged to know a lot of these people— thank you, Lord. I've known mothers and fathers, heroic in their dedication to sons and daughters. I've known the underprivileged who have refused entrance to bitterness. I've known the handicapped. Passed over as unimportant, they've used their disability as a motive, not a hindrance, to accomplishment.

● The world moves on to its final destiny, Lord, because you help so many ordinary folk to fulfill their roles in life. The world hardly notices them, but you do, Lord, just as you did long ago: "He glanced up and saw the rich putting their offerings into the treasury, and also a poor widow putting in two copper coins. At that he said: 'I assure you, this poor widow has put in more than all the rest. They make contributions out of their surplus, but she from her want has given what she could not afford—every penny she had to live on'" (Lk 21:1-4).

Sudden Death

● He sat there, perched atop the rear seat of the car. He was tanned, and handsome, and his thick hair glistened in the sun. He smiled with assurance, a man in command of his job, a man alive to the enthusiasm of the crowd. As the car moved slowly, a shot rang out. John F. Kennedy fell, and the wound was mortal.

● Lord, how quickly death can come. Let us always realize this. Let us always be prepared. We know not the year, nor the month, nor the week, nor the day, nor the hour.

● We do know, though, that you want us to so live that death will be for us a successful event: "When the corruptible frame takes on incorruptibility and the mortal immortality, then will the saying of Scripture be fulfilled: 'Death is swallowed up in victory.' 'O death, where is your victory? O death, where is your sting?'" (1 Cor 15: 54-55).

He Said It Was Too Late, Jesus

● He had been at odds with the law, Jesus. He met a girl, and fell deeply in love. Perhaps this was the first time he ever had felt deeply loved. Perhaps this was the first time he himself knew what it was to give himself in love.

● But he told her it was too late. He said his past life was too much to overcome. He said he must go his own way. Jesus, two hearts which had been gladdened by love's union, were now crushed by love's separation.

● Jesus, don't allow us ever to think our past has pre-determined our future. Despite the pain involved, let us always rise above the errors of the past. Heal the wounds caused by our wayward past, Jesus. Help us, Jesus.

She Knows Children, Jesus

● Joan is a nurse, and most of the time she's worked in the children's ward. She loves children, and knows all sorts of things about how they feel, and think, and act.

● Lord, she says we would be surprised to know how deeply children think at times. And she says they know unmistakeably whether or not adults like them and really want to be with them. She says we adults need children as much as they need us. She says that they have a lot to give us.

● Lord, I can see what being with children so much has done for Joan. It's helped make her a beautiful person. Help all of us to grow in love for children, Jesus. After all, Jesus, you yourself deeply loved children. You loved to have them close to you. You told us that we have a lot to learn from children. Lord, help us remember this.

The Prayer of an Apostle

● Jesus, each Christian is called to be an apostle for your cause. Let us imitate the spirit of St. Paul, the great apostle to the Gentiles. He tells us: "We are afflicted in every way possible, but we are not crushed; full of doubts, we never despair. We are persecuted but never abandoned; we are struck down but never destroyed. Continually we carry about in our bodies the dying of Jesus, so that in our bodies the life of Jesus may also be revealed" (2 Cor 4:8-11).

● Jesus, sometimes laboring for your cause is extremely demanding. There are long hours of work, hours which take their toll physically, mentally, and emotionally.

● Sometimes there are long hours of hidden preparation for a work of yours. The preparation seems monotonous, or tedious, or burdensome, or almost endless.

● In working for you there is sometimes little or nothing apparent in the way of results. Sometimes there is outright opposition. Sometimes, far from being appreciated, we are hated, and made fun of.

● But, Jesus, it's still a grand experience—working for you. There's nothing else like it. Because of you and your love for us, it all seems so tremendously worthwhile. The joy of it far overshadows the pain involved. Thanks, Jesus, for allowing us to help you.

Experiencing Failure

● Lord, to experience failure is part of the human condition. To feel the sting of failure is one of the ways suffering visits us. And it's a form of suffering which has its own special kind of pain.

● Jesus, failure has many different faces. There is the failure of personal relationships. This kind of failure lodges in the center of the heart. There the psyche is so sensitive, so delicate and refined in its capacity for experiencing pain. There is financial failure, which perhaps means the material ruin of a lifetime's work. And, Jesus, there can be academic failure, or various kinds of failure in the course of one's work. Lord, how painful, too, is that failure or sense of failure that can overwhelm certain parents as they helplessly watch their children go seriously astray. It may not be the parents' fault, but they can still *feel* like they have failed. Jesus, our list of different kinds of failure could go on and on....

● Jesus, help us cope properly with the pain of failure. Don't allow the hurt, the depression, the feeling of not being worth much, prevent us from struggling on. Help us grow from the experience of failure. Help us become more loving and beautiful persons precisely because we have maturely encountered failure's pain. To handle failure this way isn't easy, Jesus. But it's your way. It's the only way.

She Walks With a Limp

● Jesus, her face isn't at all attractive. And, besides, she walks with a limp. Probably no man has ever given her serious attention. If she has wanted to marry, I think to myself what a handicap she has borne. Perhaps life has been very hard for her. But, again, perhaps she has struggled and found an acceptance of herself, an inner peace, an inner happiness.

● Jesus, we all limp in one way or another. If not physically, then psychologically, mentally, morally, emotionally. In other words, Lord, none of us is perfect.

● People handle their various disabilities with varying attitudes, with varying degrees of success. Some handle the greatest disability with the greatest cheerfulness. Some grow bitter over the least disadvantage. Many face their shortcomings and try to improve, despite the sometimes tantalizingly slow pace of progress.

● Jesus, help us all. We're all burdened with ourselves in one way or the other: "Come to me, all you who are weary and find life burdensome, and I will refresh you" (Mt 11:28).

I Must Have Time for People

● Lord, you had time for people when you lived among us. And I don't just mean people gathered in great big crowds. You gave yourself this way, too. But you also gave yourself to individuals. When others would pass by uncaringly, you would take time for an individual. And often you seemed to take special interest in a person considered to be a nobody.

● Like the time you came across the man at the Pool of Bethesda, where sick people gathered to be cured at the stirring of the water: "There was one man who had been sick for thirty-eight years. Jesus, who knew he had been sick a long time, said when he saw him lying there, 'Do you want to be healed?' 'Sir,' the sick man answered, 'I do not have anyone to plunge me into the pool once the water has been stirred up. By the time I get there, someone else has gone in ahead of me.' Jesus said to him, 'Stand up! Pick up your mat and walk!' The man was immediately cured; he picked up his mat and began to walk" (Jn 5:5-9).

● Jesus, sometimes I tell myself I'm too busy for this or that individual. I know there's a lot to do, and only so many hours in a day. But sometimes I'm kidding myself. People are what your work is all about. I have to have time for people—and individual people. This is the way you acted.

● Each individual is precious to you, Jesus. Each one has been touched by your redemptive blood. Help me always to remember this, Jesus.

A Loved One Is Suffering

● Jesus, one of the great big sufferings in life is to see a loved one in pain.

● A loved one can lie on a sick bed, in pain, in a loneliness we cannot relieve, in terminal illness. And we hurt, too.

● A loved one has special problems—failure in work, unjust treatment, financial difficulty, a seeming inability to contact God. And we hurt, too.

● A loved one can occasionally feel overwhelmed by life. At such times, to live seems so difficult, so frustrating, so demanding, so painful. And we hurt, too.

● Lord, when a loved one is suffering, enlighten us, show us what to do. Always allow us to be very kind, and understanding, and supportive, and loving.

I've Avoided You, Jesus

● Jesus, sometimes you've looked at me, inviting me to talk things over with you, but I've kind of avoided you. Not entirely—we remained friends, but I was unwilling to really discuss a certain point with you.

● I was afraid to let you enter my life fully on a certain issue. I wasn't doing anything really wrong—but I wanted pretty much to control the activity or attitude all by myself. I was afraid to discuss the matter in an in-depth way with you—I was afraid you'd ask me to change.

● Jesus, let me see how silly I am when I act like this. You love me tremendously, I know, and you only want the best for me. Why should I be afraid to talk things over with you? Why should I be afraid no matter what you ask of me?

● Help me, Jesus. Help me to be always open with you. Deep down I really want you to come into my life more and more. I don't want any part of it to be a closed area to you. Help me, Jesus.

Humility Is Truth

●   Lord, the Old Testament tells us:

Humble yourself the more, the
     greater you are,
     and you will find favor with God.
For great is the power of God;
       by the humble he is glorified.

(Sir 3:18-19)

●   Jesus, we have a tendency to attribute our talents and accomplishments to ourselves.

●   We have a part in the good we do, but you have the greater part. Without you we can do nothing.

●   Jesus, humility is truth. It is recognizing our good points and our bad points. It is thanking you for helping us to be good. It is a willingness to work against our failings.

●   Jesus, let us see what humility really is. Let us see that courage, strength, and even great accomplishments are in no way opposed to humility, but rather enhanced by it. Let us see that there's something especially beautiful about a really humble person.

Lord, Life Is Not Always Neat and Tidy

● Lord, at times we try to lay out life in neatly cut pieces that fit together perfectly. The only problem is that life most often is not this way. Life is far from always being neat and tidy.

● We expect the people we deal with to act in a certain way—in a sort of programmed way we have worked out for them in our own minds. But people can be vastly mysterious and free—often they don't react the way we had expected.

● And the way our work goes, Lord—this can take crazy and surprising turns along the road of life. Not to realize this is to invite frustration and disappointment.

● We are often surprised at our inner lives, too, Jesus. We can neatly map out the way we want to follow you. But how often the path twists and turns unexpectedly.

● Lord, help me to be flexible enough to meet the unexpected properly. Instill within me a suppleness that will allow me to cope correctly with the untidiness of life.

He's Out for Money, Jesus

● Jesus, he admits it. He says his one big aim in life is to make a lot of money.

● He's not the first one to think like this, Lord. But it's really a shame to waste the beauty of a human life on the inordinate pursuit of material gain, Jesus.

● A human life is so precious, intended for expressions of true grandeur—loving another in a special way; being loved; giving oneself in a selfless service to the family of man; struggling to accomplish what is truly human, and then experiencing a sense of satisfaction; enjoying the breathless beauty of God's creation—these are a few of the things worthy of a human life, Jesus.

● How sad, Jesus, that some waste the precious reality which is life on that which is unworthy of human endeavor. Lord, you once told a parable about a man who hoarded material possessions: "But God said to him, 'You fool! This very night your life shall be required of you. To whom will all this piled-up wealth of yours go?' That is the way it works with the man who grows rich for himself instead of growing rich in the sight of God" (Lk 12:20-21).

Misunderstandings

● Lord, to experience a certain amount of misunderstanding is inevitable. Sometimes we bring it on ourselves. Sometimes others are to blame. Sometimes nobody in particular is to blame—it just happens.

● We can be misunderstood in good times—when all is well. Then it doesn't hurt so much, even though a loved one is involved.

● We can be misunderstood in bad times—when things are going wrong. Then the hurt goes deep—why do we have to endure one more pain now?

● Lord, no matter what the cause, no matter who is involved, no matter what my condition, let me profit from times of misunderstanding. Don't let me sulk, don't let me complain, don't let me feel persecuted. You experienced misunderstanding, too, Jesus. Let me remember this.

People Are In a Hurry, Lord

● It's funny, Lord, but a lot of times it seems we're in a great big hurry, but really going no place.

● People rush around on the downtown streets going to a big sale to buy things they really don't need.

● The man in the big limousine is speeding home from the office so he can hurry up and rush off to a social event which he's really not interested in. But if he doesn't go, he thinks it might hurt his social status, which, by the way, is costing him a lot of money. So he ends up spending a lot of money so he can go to parties and dinners which really bore him. It's kind of crazy, isn't it, Jesus?

● Other people pack their families in a car, and go off on a cross country vacation. At each spot they stop, they find themselves in a hurry to get on to the next site. And this is a vacation, Lord?

● I guess all of us do our share of rushing about for no real purpose, Jesus. Help us see that life isn't basically a matter of going here and there, doing this and that. Life is primarily a matter of being—of being the persons you want us to be. If we are what we're supposed to be, then our doing and moving about will have a real meaning.

You Have To Give It To Keep It

● Jesus, I recently heard a man give a talk about the Christian life, especially about love. He said, "You have to give it to keep it."

● Lord, I think in his own way he was saying what you yourself have told us: "Whoever would save his life will lose it, and whoever loses his life for my sake will save it" (Lk 9:24).

● Your saying is a constant challenge to us, Jesus, a daily challenge. Each day we have to break through that shell of selfishness which would have us live only for ourselves.

● Sometimes we feel the pain of giving ourselves, Jesus. Sometimes it's the pain of the physical weariness in serving others. Sometimes it's the pain of criticism, a criticism arising precisely because we are trying to be for others—but in a way some do not approve of. Sometimes it's the pain of disinterestedness shown us. Sometimes it's the pain of fighting lethargy.

● But despite the pain, we have to keep giving ourselves in love, Jesus. It's the only way to live. You yourself said so.

●   Lord, long ago the prophet Amos said:

Hear this, you who trample upon the
    needy
      and destroy the poor of the land!

(Am 8:4)

●   Today, Lord, those words are just as necessary as they were then. There are all sorts of social injustices—with all sorts of visible scars. The scars are there for all of us to see—if only we are willing to look. There are the bloated bellies of starving children, the filth and disease of poverty, the despair written on the face of the world's disinherited.

●   Lord, we who say we hate the sins of injustice have to do something. We can't merely bemoan the situation, wringing our hands, yet inactive. We all can do something. What should I be doing, Lord?

I Wasn't Very Nice, Lord

● Lord, I wasn't very nice to him. I got mad and said things I shouldn't have. I'm sorry, Lord. I told him, too, that I was sorry.

● Jesus, we all have faults and failings. Once we fail, the only thing to do is to admit it, and be sorry. We also have to try to learn from our mistakes.

● Lord, there is one fault I especially want you to keep me from. That's refusing to admit that I have faults. I know how you feel about such an attitude: "The Pharisee with head unbowed prayed in this fashion: 'I give you thanks, O God, that I am not like the rest of men—grasping, crooked, adulterous—or even like this tax collector'" (Lk 18:11). Lord, in this parable you went on to say that the tax collector admitted being a sinner and asked God's mercy, and that he "went home from the temple justified but the other did not" (Lk 18:14).

● Thank you, Lord, for that story. It tells us a lot.

My Father's Will

● Jesus, Scripture has given us these words of yours: "None of those who cry out, 'Lord, Lord,' will enter the kingdom of God but only the one who does the will of my Father in heaven" (Mt 7:21).

● Jesus, sometimes I know I'm not nearly conscious enough of the Father's will. I don't always allow it to penetrate my existence as I should. I should be more aware of the Father's will as it wants to guide me in all the ordinary happenings of everydayness.

● Jesus, help me to imitate you in the love you had for your Father's will. It was your consuming desire to accomplish that will in the greatest undertakings, as well as in the smallest matters. The Father's will was your greatest joy, but it also meant your anguished and bloody death. But you did not flinch, you did not falter.

● Help me, Jesus, to let the Father's will transform me more and more. At times his will may mean the deepest suffering, but it also means the deepest and greatest happiness.

Some Think It's a Lousy World, Jesus

● Lord, some people think this is a pretty messed up world. They say it's a lousy world. They say things aren't going to get any better, either. They say there's no use expecting kindness or help of any kind. If some of this comes your way, these people say it's kind of like an accident.

● Lord, these people aren't all agreed about how to live in what seems to them to be a lousy world. Some become ruthless, and trample over everybody and everything. Some center their lives on sex, or drink, or drugs, saying that a person has to squeeze quick pleasure as often as he can out of this messed up world. Some become bitter. Some become indifferent and say they don't give a damn about anything. Some court despair.

● Jesus, I think the majority of people feel otherwise. They realize there's a lot wrong with the world. But they believe the only sensible attitude is to work to make things better. They admit that greed and hatred and lust and all kinds of injustice hold a strongly fortressed position in the world. But they believe that love and kindness and generosity and hope are even stronger.

● Jesus, give a sense of hope to those who despair

of the world. Give a sense of strength to those who believe in the world's basic goodness. Amid the pain of the human condition, inspire them to continue their efforts to make things better. Assist them in helping clear away the debris of the world's sinfulness, a debris which clouds the true image of man's world—an image of truth, and goodness, and beauty.

With My Family

●   Lord, I love to be with my family. There is only my Mother and Sister now. My Father has gone home to you, but the memory of him keeps Dad with us in all sorts of ways.

●   I love to just sit and talk with Mother. She's eighty-two now, and physically growing weaker. But her mind is sharp and alert, and I thank you especially for this, Lord. She's a wonderful person, so gentle, and so motherly-wise. She's taught me an awful lot over the years, Jesus.

●   My Sister, Merle, is such a good person. She takes wonderful care of Mother, Jesus. She's hard-working, and she values the right things in life. I've come to appreciate her more as the years go on. Lord, be with her and love her in a special way.

●   Lord, you loved your family life, too. You loved to be with Mary and Joseph. Thanks so much, Jesus, for family life. Help me always realize what a great gift it really is.

A Baseball Game

● Lord, it's good to be here watching the ball game with my friends, Ed and Bill. It's a colorful setting. The green of the playing field is surrounded by seats of blue, green, yellow, and red. Vendors roam the aisles selling peanuts, and popcorn, and beer, and soda pop.

● The field is dotted with players—professionals, major league players, the best in their sport. The fans applaud their skill. The players go all out—they want to win, they get paid to win.

● Jesus, St. Paul drew from the world of sports in talking about the Christian life: "You know that while all the runners in the stadium take part in the race, the award goes to one man. In that case, run so as to win! Athletes deny themselves all sorts of things. They do this to win a crown of leaves that withers, but we a crown that is imperishable" (1 Cor 9:24-25).

● Lord, just as athletes are willing to put forth the necessary effort to excel, help me work at being a good Christian. Don't allow me to surrender to that temptation which suggests, "It's all too hard—this business of being Christian. Why try so hard? Why bother? Why not relax and enjoy life in the easiest possible way? Why sweat it?"

● Jesus, I want to resist that temptation. Help me, Jesus.

The Power of Our Words

● Lord, our words carry a great capacity for good or evil. They can build up, or they can tear down.

● To one in agonizing grief, a sympathetic word can be a tower of strength. To one who has worked well and hard, a word of praise can be an encouragement to greater things. To one in error, a sincere admonishment can prevent further straying.

● And the misuse of words—there are many possibilities here, too. How often a cutting word has further wounded an already bruised heart. How often a person's reputation has been unjustly damaged. How often divisive words have helped to destroy community. How often unjust criticism has thwarted possibilities for good.

● Yes, Lord, the use of speech is a capacity for great good or great evil. In the Epistle of St. James the tongue is spoken of: "We use it to say, 'Praised be the Lord and Father'; then we use it to curse men, though they are made in the likeness of God. Blessing and curse come out of the same mouth" (Jas 3:9-10).

● Jesus, help our words be constructive, prevent their being destructive.

Rush-Hour Traffic

● The cars move slowly, almost bumper to bumper. They're in all shades of blues and greens and reds and tans and other colors. Inside the cars there are all sorts of people—men and women and teen-agers, rich executives, white collar workers, and common laborers.

● Lord, rush-hour traffic is verging on the impossible. The number of cars seems to increase, and the road space seems always to be shrinking. When I'm driving at this time, I really have to work at keeping patient. A dog-eat-dog attitude is strong, if not prevalent. I'm tempted to make this attitude my own.

● But I know this isn't your way, Lord. Your way would have me be kind and courteous in the heavy traffic. This courtesy is a little way of showing Christian love for my neighbor. It seems like a little thing, Lord, but the seemingly insignificant ways of showing love and respect are important. If we sat back and waited for the big and grand opportunities, we wouldn't love very often.

● Most of the people I encounter on the road I'll never see again. But still, Lord, they are my neighbors.

Moments of Silence

●   Lord, there are moments of silence in nature. There is the stillness of a lake on a summer's eve, as the sun settles quietly upon the horizon. There is the striking silence of the mountains, majestic and so mighty, yet reaching ever so quietly into the sky. There is the meadow in springtime, alive with a fresh greenness, yet quiet—there is only the stir of a gentle breeze.

●   Lord, you have put this quest for silence in the lakes and the mountains and the meadows. You have also put a quest for silence within me—within all men.

●   Lord, we need moments of silence to reflect and pray about ourselves, about our relationship to others and the whole of creation. Authentic silence is taking the time to reflect on what it means to exist, on what it means to love, on what it means to be for you, and for others.

●   Jesus, we need moments of silence to look at you, to drink in your goodness, your kindness, your gentleness, your strength, your mercy, and your love. We need to look at you and revitalize our thinking, rooting it more in your way of life. We need to look at you and refurbish our desire to give all we've got—for you, and for those for whom you died.

●   Jesus, help us to be silent.

You Have Called Me, and You Are Calling Me, Jesus

● Lord, as I sit here reading my Bible, I come across these words: "As he was walking along the Sea of Galilee he watched two brothers, Simon now known as Peter, and his brother Andrew, casting a net into the sea. They were fishermen. He said to them, 'Come after me and I will make you fishers of men.' They immediately abandoned their nets and became his followers" (Mt 4:18-20).

● Jesus, you have not only called the Apostles to carry on your work. You have also called me. You have called all Christians.

● Your call is a privilege, Lord. Help me always to be aware of this. Your call is a responsibility, Lord. Help me to live up to this.

● Your call is not a one-time thing, Jesus. Each day you are before me, calling me anew, challenging me to that which I have not yet achieved, encouraging me, comforting me, strengthening me. Help me to realize this, Jesus—everyday.

● Sometimes I have answered your call reluctantly, Jesus, sometimes with enthusiasm. Sometimes, answering your call has meant a lot of suffering. Sometimes answering your call has meant a lot of fun, a sharing in camaraderie, a special feeling that it was good for us to be there.

● Lord, thanks for calling me. Please keep on calling me. Help me always answer with a freshness, with a quiet if not always vivacious enthusiasm. Help me answer with courage amid distress, with humility amid success, with faith, and hope, and love.

The City at Night

● The city is alive this Saturday night. The neon lights flash on and off, inviting people to movies, to cocktail lounges, to restaurants, and to adult peep-shows.

● Lord, the people downtown tonight have different motives. Some are bent on sin. Others want to have a good time while respecting your laws.

● There is the morally callous man, suave and handsome, out with another man's wife. He's dining her, he's flattering her, he is building her up for his only real intent—at the night's end he wants to have sex.

● There are others like him, Lord, each out for sin in his or her own way.

● But there are good people in town tonight, too, Lord. There's the man who is showing his wife a good time. She's been at home all week, cooking, washing dishes, making beds. Tonight's dinner and movie are a refresher for her. It's one way her husband says thank you.

● There are other decent people here tonight, too, Lord. Some are vivaciously young, some are middle-aged, a few are serenely old.

● Jesus, be with all who are in the city tonight. Inspire the good to remain good. Sway those with evil intent from their sinful ways. Reassure the good that entertainment taken according to your will is the only kind which really refreshes. Let those bent on evil see that the short-lived pleasure of sin never really satisfies.

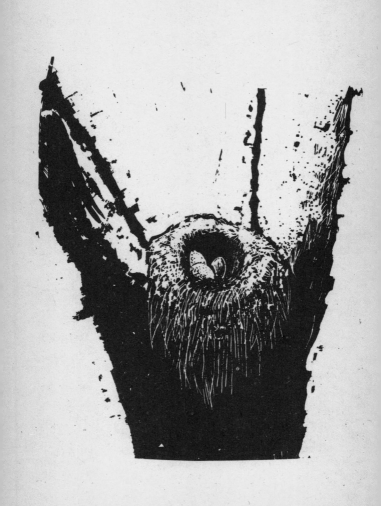

Many Different Gifts

● Jesus, each of us has his own gift, his own task, his own mission to fulfill: "There are different gifts but the same Spirit; there are different ministries but the same Lord; there are different works but the same God who accomplishes all of them in everyone" (1 Cor 12:4-6).

● Jesus, keep each of us enlightened as to his task. Keep us inspired to work at it. Keep us strengthend to see it through.

● Lord, some tasks appear outwardly important. Others seem to be not important at all. But any task you put before us, Lord, is important—precisely because it is you who ask its accomplishment.

● Jesus, none of us can accomplish another's task. We can help each other, encourage each other, stand side by side. But the task itself is each one's alone. Each has the privilege and responsibility of fulfilling his unique mission, his unique task. Jesus, help us always to be aware of this.

The Human Body

● Lord, the human body was created good, very good. You added to its holiness in becoming man:

The Word became flesh....

(Jn 1:14)

● Lord, men have not always respected the holiness of the body. They have abused its sacredness. They have committed all sorts of foul deeds through it. Through the body men have murdered, maimed, raped, committed adultery, lied, robbed, slandered, blasphemed, wallowed in drunkenness, courted hedonism.

● Lord, through your grace men have also allowed the body's holiness to be manifest. Through the body man and wife have deeply loved. Through the body mothers have nursed their infants. Through the body encouraging smiles have uplifted the downhearted. Through the body words of encouragement have been a catalyst for great accomplishment. Through the body men have heroically proven, in all sorts of ways, that they do love their brothers, even though the proof is the laying down of life itself.

● Jesus, help us to realize always the holiness of our bodies. Help us not to desecrate them. Help us to use our bodies to express the good, and the true, and the beautiful.

A "Joy Killing"

● Jesus, I read a sad, sad story in this morning's paper. The story told how a four-year-old girl was playing in a neighbor's yard. A car containing several men drove past. A shot-gun blast rang out. The little, precious, innocent, helpless girl fell dead to the ground.

● The police authorities say it seemed to be a "joy-killing"—no apparent motive. They just did it for fun. Is this true, Lord? Unless they were drugged, or drunk, or insane, could these men have committed such an act? Could they have done it knowingly, in cold blood, just for the fun of it?

● If they did it just for the fun of it, what does this say about our society, Lord? Jesus, if these men are guilty of this horrendous crime, do all of us have to ask ourselves whether we are to blame in some way for our present state of things?

● Lord, I think the sins committed against your little children must have weighed especially heavy upon your broken heart as, contemplating them, you hung upon the cross. You loved them so: "People were bringing their little children to him to have him touch them, but the disciples were scolding them for this. Jesus became indignant when he noticed it and said to them: 'Let the children come to me and do not hinder them. It is to just such as these that the kingdom of God belongs'" (Mk 10:13-14).

The Choice Is Ours

● Life is ours, Jesus, to do with it what we choose.

● We can use it for all sorts of selfish pursuits. We can use it to make others give us attention and acclaim. We can use life mainly as an opportunity to enjoy illicit sex. We can use it to cheat our brother. We can use it to hoard wealth, and harden our hearts against cries of hunger. We can use it, waste it, in the pursuit of all sorts of silly status symbols. We can use it, waste it, in the desire for myriad experiences unworthy of a human being.

● We can also use life, Jesus, in all sorts of beautiful ways. We can use it everyday to be kind, especially to people who are little thought of, who are ugly, who are sick, who are overwhelmingly lonely.

● We can use life to love—to love tenderly and coura- geously, and with a desire to suffer to accomplish love's tasks.

● Lord, we can use life to accomplish our small but important part in the building of a better world where there will be less hatred and more love, less war and more peace, less racism and more equal opportunity for all, less materialism and greater emphasis upon spiritual values, less rejection of you, Jesus, and a growing desire to love you, and to serve you.

● Jesus, life is before us. We can use it the way we choose. You are there to help us use it correctly, for we cannot use life properly without you. But the choice is ours. You will not force our wills. Ecclesiasticus tells us:

> If you choose you can keep the
>   commandments;
> it is loyalty to do his will.
> There are set before you fire and
>   water;
> to whichever you choose, stretch
>   forth your hand.
> Before man are life and death,
>   whichever he chooses shall be given
>   him.

(Sir 15:15-17)

A Restaurant

● Lord, as I sit in the restaurant, I see a variety of people. There is the elderly couple, off at a side table. They seem serenely at home with each other. There is a family of five—father, mother, a teen-aged daughter, and two young boys. They're obviously happy—happy with their togetherness. There's a young couple in a side booth, sort of oblivious to the surroundings. They seem engrossed in their love of perhaps recent bloom.

● Lord, a meal is such a common denominator kind of experience. People of all ages and interests enjoy breaking bread with their friends and other loved ones.

● You, too, Jesus, liked to eat with friends. There was, of course, the Last Supper. But there were many other times also. Thanks, Lord, for the warm, familiar experience of eating together.

He Will Soon Die, Lord

● The doctor's diagnosis came suddenly, without warning, with a kind of resounding finality. Jack, the brother of my friend, Grace, has leukemia, and without the touch of the miraculous, he will soon depart from us.

● Lord, happenings like this leave loved ones with a complex set of emotions. There is grief at the impending loss, a feeling of helplessness, an aching feeling which reaches deep down to the sensitive core of one's capacity to suffer. Yet for the believer, there is still a pervading desire for abandonment to God's providence.

● Jesus, deep as is suffering at a time like this, how much worse it would be without you. How utterly terrible would it be to lose one so dearly loved if it weren't for faith—faith in you, faith in what you have told us about life's purpose, about death, about eternal life. Thanks, Jesus, for yourself and your message:

> I am the resurrection and the life:
> whoever believes in me,
> though he should die, will come to
> life;
> and whoever is alive and believes in
> me
> will never die.

(Jn 11:25-26)

Country People and City People

● Lord, city people seem to live so differently than country people.

● Urban people live in densely populated areas, where it is sort of difficult to be alone. Stores are crowded and streets are crowded. At work a person's office space may only be a few square feet. A person's house may be separated from a neighbor's by only a few arm's lengths. And there are many things to do, many places to go, many sights to see. For many people, urban life, despite its frustrations, has a lot going for it.

● It's different in the country, Lord. People there live in an expansive setting. Fields and rolling meadows surround one's home rather than other houses. The business district may consist of only a few shops and stores and buildings. People live a relatively simple existence. There are not too many different things to do, nor places to go, nor sights to see. But the more ordinary experiences of country people, precisely because they are free of all sorts of trappings, can be exquisite in their very simplicity.

● Yet are country people and city people really that

much different, Lord? True, their external existences are much in contrast. But deep down in the core of their beings they are the same. They have the same basic needs. Whether a person lives in the country or the city he needs to love and to be loved. He wants to find satisfaction and success in his work. He wants to feel useful and needed. He wants to be accepted by others. Lord, these are some of the ways country people and city people are the same. Jesus, help us all to fulfill these human needs according to your will.

We Have to Pay the Price, Jesus

● Lord, your apostle Paul suffered a lot for his commitment to you: "Five times at the hands of the Jews I received forty lashes less one; three times I was beaten with rods; I was stoned once, shipwrecked three times; I passed a day and a night on the sea. I travelled continually, endangered by floods, robbers, my own people, the Gentiles; imperiled in the city, in the desert, at sea..." (2 Cor 11:24-26).

● Jesus, we may not have to suffer what Paul did. But if we are serious about our commitment to you, we have to pay the price in one way or the other.

● We have to pay the price in the various ways put forth by your teaching.

● We have to love our enemies when our feelings tempt us to hate them.

● We have to struggle with our tendency to selfishness, day in and day out. We have to be aware of all the ways selfishness wants to show itself—sometimes very open-ly, sometimes so subtly, so hiddenly.

● We have to take the trouble to be really concerned about the poor, the racially oppressed, the sick, the lonely.

● We have to put forth the effort to control our sex-uality, Jesus. It's a beautiful gift when used according to your designs. But there is a lot of temptation in today's world which entices a person to desecrate your gift, Jesus. We have to pay the price, Lord.

● Jesus, we have to pay the price in being true to our daily task. Work at times can be boring, wearying, frustrating, demanding, disappointing, lonely.

● There are all sorts of ways through which the price is asked of us, Jesus—the price of following you. But what we suffer, Jesus, is so small compared to what your love for us deserves. St. Paul knew this. Jesus, help us also to know it.

Resurrection Joy

● It happened one morning, a long, long time ago: "On the first day of the week, at dawn, the women came to the tomb bringing the spices they had prepared. They found the stone rolled back from the tomb; but when they entered the tomb, they did not find the body of the Lord Jesus" (Lk 24:1-3).

● Thanks, Jesus, for your resurrection.

● Lord, let me always remember that your resurrection is a sign of your victory. You have overcome, and overcome forever. Nothing—no event, no person, no organized effort, can rob you of what is eternally yours.

● Lord, no matter how dark things become at times, let me realize that I really can't lose—unless I let go of you. You're with me—you who have won once and for all, you who rose from the dead, you who share your victory with me.

● Jesus, let resurrection joy, your resurrection joy, surround my life, penetrate my life, direct my life.

● Thanks, Jesus, for your resurrection.

We Can Feel Insecure, Lord

●   Lord, it's human to have feelings of insecurity. All of us in various ways, at various times, in various circumstances, for various reasons, feel insecure.

●   Some feel insecure because of physical ordinariness, or even ugliness.

●   Some feel insecure because they're not very smart, and sometimes they feel stupid and ashamed.

●   Some feel insecure because their personalities seem to others so ordinary, or even drab. They try to improve, but the change is so slow, so difficult.

●   Some feel insecure because no one seems to really love them, or really care. This is a real painful kind of insecurity, Lord.

●   Some feel insecure in their work, Lord. They don't feel comfortable with their jobs. They don't feel on top of things. Their work anxiety can gnaw at the stomach, fray the nerves, make life hard and miserable.

●   Lord, whatever our kind of insecurity, help us all. Make us feel more secure. Let us feel more the warmth of your love, the strength of your hand, the reassuring smile of your manly face.

Idols Instead of God

● As I read my Bible, I come to Hosea the prophet. He has moving words about God and His beloved Israel:

> When Israel was a child I loved him,
>   out of Egypt I called my son.
> The more I called them,
>   the farther they went from me,
> Sacrificing to the Baals
>   and burning incense to idols.
> Yet it was I who taught Ephraim to
>   walk,
>   who took them in my arms....

(Hos 11:1-3)

● Lord, we, too, can reject God's love—your love, the Spirit's love, the Father's love.

● Jesus, you love us tenderly, constantly, mightily, lavishly. Help us not to refuse your love, Lord. Do not allow us to set up false idols in place of you.

● We can become our own idols—making ourselves, not you, the focus of attention.

● There are all sorts of idols possible to us, Jesus—greed, selfishness, pride, unconcern for our brothers, promiscuous sex, gluttony, laziness, and many more.

● Jesus, help us keep these idols out of our lives. Let us see them for what they really are—obstacles to your love getting through to us, obstacles to our loving you.

If Only . . .

● Lord, I have to watch out that I don't become an "if only" kind of person. We're all tempted to this sort of attitude.

● We can have this "if only" attitude about so many persons and things and life situations. We tell ourselves if only this or that were not so, if only things were more this way, or less this way, well, yes, *then* we would be better and more effective Christians.

● We can give out with all sorts of "if only's," Jesus. We can say if only it weren't so difficult to pray sometimes, then we would pray better and more often . . . if only more people gave us a better Christian witness, then we could be more committed Christians . . . if only the world were more God-conscious, then we could find Him more easily . . . if only others would love us more, then we would love more, too . . . .

● Jesus, help us to learn to look more at what actually *is* about ourselves, about our present work, about others, about all the various situations and circumstances of our here and now existences. Keep us from becoming "if only" kind of people.

To Whom Would I Go, Lord?

●   Jesus, I feel just like Peter did: "Jesus then said to the Twelve, 'Do you want to leave me too?' Simon Peter answered him, 'Lord, to whom shall we go? You have the words of eternal life'" (Jn 6:67-68).

●   There have been all sorts of leaders throughout history, Lord. They have espoused all sorts of causes. They have passed, perhaps their causes have, too. Their followers are no more.

●   But with you it's different, Jesus. You and your cause still remain. You are alive, your cause is alive. You still stir the hearts of millions of men, and women, and children from all walks of life.

●   Lord, I can't imagine life without you. What would I do without you? Without you, what real meaning would there be to my life? Without you there would be a profound emptiness, a massive emptiness, an emptiness impossible to fill.

●   Thanks, Jesus, for revealing yourself to us. Thanks for revealing yourself to me. You alone have the answer to the mystery of life. You alone have the message of eternal life.

The Heights and the Depths

● Jesus, during a life-time we experience all kinds of emotional states. We have moderate ups and downs. Then, there are a lot of times when we feel emotionally even, in a kind of quiet sort of way.

● Sometimes, though, Jesus, we can feel the extremes of emotional states—deep depression, or grief, and ecstatic joy and happiness.

● Jesus, deep grief can leave our whole being feeling limp and almost helpless. Deep depression can eat away at our innermost core, making us feel far from joy, far from being interested in either work or play, far from eagerly welcoming another day.

● Lord, we can have moments of ecstatic happiness, too. Whatever the cause, we feel completely alive—all over, and deep down, down in the innermost depths where we are most ourselves.

● Jesus, whether we're feeling happy, or sad, quietly serene, vibrant with joy, weighed with grief—or however, be with us. Help us be as we're supposed to be amid the myriad possibilities of feeling this way or that.

The Home for Old People

● Jesus, the home for old people I visited is like a lot of other ones, I guess. In most of these the food is about the same, there are the same kinds of nurses and attendants, the rooms are about the same size and similarly furnished.

● But, Jesus, there are differences, too. Each of the old folks is different, each a unique individual. As they grow older, and gradually approach closer and closer to their final day, each one has a unique situation to live with. Some, each in his or her own way, are worried about their numbered days. Some of them want to die, yet are afraid to die. Others serenely look forward to meeting you, and their peace and charm are breathlessly beautiful. There are other differences, too, Jesus. You know all about them.

● Jesus, help me be especially kind to old people. In many ways they become increasingly dependent upon us, we who are not yet old ourselves, but who one day, sooner than we think, will be burdened with the problems which are now theirs. There is something so inspiring, Jesus, about persons, who, despite the burdens of the aged, grow old gracefully. Jesus, let me help the aged in my own small way to achieve this graciousness of advancing years.

The Gifts of Creation

● The Book of Wisdom speaks to us of God:

> For you love all things that are
>   and loathe nothing that you have
>   made;
>   for what you hated, you would not
>   have fashioned.
> And how could a thing remain, unless
>   you willed it;
>   or be preserved, had it not been
>   called forth by you?

(Wis 11:24-25)

● Lord, you love what you have made, and you surround us with the gifts of your creation. Thank you, Lord.

● When we use creation properly, Jesus, we grow, we become more mature. We become more human. We become better Christians.

● Lord, we don't always use your created gifts properly. We can misuse them in all sorts of ways. When we do, we think we're going to reap some sort of benefit. This is really silly, Lord. How can we expect to profit by abusing your gifts of love? If we misuse creation, to that extent our growth is stunted. We become less human, less Christian. Help us, Jesus, to remember this.

Jesus, We Can Flee Responsibility

● Lord, bearing responsibility is not always pleasant. A lot of times we are tempted to cop out, as the saying goes.

● There's a long list of stories of how people can cop out, Jesus. Thousands of husbands and fathers have deserted their families. Many others have neglected job responsibilities, or Church responsibilities.

● We can flee responsibilities in more subtle ways, too, Jesus. We can refuse opportunities to become more what you want us to be. We can be irresponsible in neglecting occasions for being kind, and understanding, and loving.

● Jesus, help us to resist the temptation of fleeing responsibility. Help us realize that to be a mature Christian means the willingness to accept responsibility, painful as this may sometimes be. And thanks, Jesus, for your help in the past.

Jesus, You're the One Way

● Jesus, at a recent revival, they developed a slogan about you. The slogan is "The One Way." They're talking about you, Jesus. That slogan says a lot, Lord.

● Jesus, the Father has spoken to us through you completely, definitively, irrevocably: "In times past, God spoke in fragmentary and varied ways to our fathers through the prophets; in this, the final age, he has spoken to us through his Son..." (Heb 1:1-2).

● The Father has spoken through you, Jesus, and still speaks through you. He wants us to look at you, to study you, to reflect on your attitude toward life, to follow in your footsteps, to love you mightily, to realize that you love us mightily, too.

● Jesus, you are human and divine. When we look at you as man, Jesus, what do we see? We see a man who redeemed us within the framework of a human life. You did not reject the human condition, but embraced it eagerly with your whole manhood, living within it, rejoicing because of it, suffering because of it. St. Paul says of you:

Though he was in the form of God,
   he did not deem equality with God
   something to be grasped at.
Rather, he emptied himself
   and took the form of a slave,
   being born in the likeness of men.

(Phil 2:6-7)

●   Thanks, Jesus, for living as a man among us. Thanks for showing us the way to the Father. Thanks for being "The One Way."

response in CHRIST
a study of the Christian life

Edward Carter, S.J.

103 — RESPONSE IN CHRIST — A Study of the Christian Life   1.45 ppr

A masterful blend of current-day spirituality and the authentic, essential and unchanging elements which have constantly inserted themselves throughout the history of Christian spirituality.

109 — THE SPIRIT IS PRESENT
by Edward Carter   1.25 ppr
Hard cover edition   5.95

Christian spirituality concerns itself with our total human life lived in Christ under the guidance of the Spirit. We can, then, immediately see one of the root meanings of the terms spirituality and spiritual life.

121 — NOW IS THE TIME
by Edward Carter, S.J.   1.45 ppr.

A "prayer starter," an aid to personal meditation, based on the Bible. Useful to groups engaged in shared prayer. An inspiration to happiness and optimism.

**THE JESUS EXPERIENCE by Edward Car-
ter, S.J.** — The "institutional" Church
may be in difficulties, but its Founder,
Jesus, is riding the crest of a new wave
of popularity. In this age, avid for
"experiences," Fr. Carter writes mov-
ingly of the one experience which pro-
duces permanent effects: meeting Jesus.

$1.75

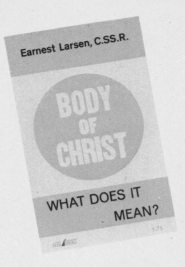

Earnest Larsen, C.SS.R.

BODY
OF
CHRIST

WHAT DOES IT
MEAN?

1.75

BODY OF CHRIST by Earnest Larsen, C.SS.R. — Splendid, modern reflections, enriched by apt illustrations, on the everyday reality of the Eucharistic Sacrament which is inseparably linked to the flesh and blood Sacrifice of Calvary and which the author with great sensitivity leads us to find as surely in the tenement as in the Tabernacle.

$1.75

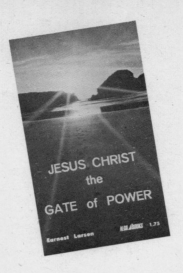

JESUS CHRIST, THE GATE OF POWER by
Earnest Larsen, C.SS.R. — meeting with
Jesus is like falling in love with the girl
next door: you have always known her
— and Him — and yet . . . birds begin to
sing in the treetops, white clouds sail
across the sky and tomorrow is going to
be a splendid day!

Fr. Larsen writes beautifully about Jesus
the REALITY — not Jesus the RITE, which
is what most of us experience. We know
ABOUT Jesus but we seldom KNOW
HIM. What do "Savior," "Community,"
"Baptism," "Redemption" and other familiar words signify? Read the profound
and sensitive replies to these and many
other questions in this fine volume.

$1.75

[SE]XUALITY SUMMARY by William J. [Al]len, J.C.D. — After all the debate [an]d discussion of the past ten years, [ho]w much do people really KNOW [ab]out sexual morality? Have there [be]en any new developments? How do [yo]u "form your conscience"? Has the ["a]nything goes" principle become re-[sp]ectable?

[He]re is a clear, coherent, convincing [an]d compassionate picture of four main [pr]oblem areas: homosexuality, abor-[tio]n, contraception and premarital sex.
[It] outlines the best modern thinking [on] these areas and the solutions pro-[po]sed. Fully updated and complete [wi]th extensive Bibliography for fur-[th]er reading, it is the most practical [w]ork on this subject to appear in many [ye]ars. **$1.75**

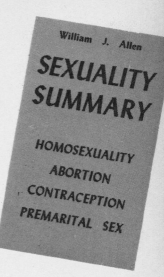

I SEARCH AT ODD ANGLES by James Goedken — Books of prayer are avail-able, but how many of them have been written with High School students in mind?

This one has. It is immersed in life and speaks of life. These Scripture-based prayers have been formulated for his students by Fr. Goedken day by day over several years.

Divided into Themes like Thanking, Loving, Wondering, Listening, Believ-ing and many others, this book of prayers will be found just right for School Assemblies, Youth Groups, Pray-er Groups and, not least, for family prayer. **$1.75**

WELCOME, NUMBER 4,000,000,000! by James V. Schall, S.J. — Christianity has been accused of being the root cause of population and ecology problems. Yet the lesson of history is that the number of men the planet can support is not limited to existing resources; it depends mostly on human creativity which is the supreme resource. As long as there is no limit to human knowledge, there is no effective limit to what knowledge can accomplish.

Fr. Schall treats of politics, environment and technology in our time, studying each of these in the light of Christian principles. His book will be welcomed by the intelligent reader dissatisfied with conventional wisdom, and it will be found especially useful by students of these problems.

145 — ISBN O — 8189 — 114 $1.75

WORKING WITH PARISH COUNCILS? by William J. Rademacher — Fr. Rademacher brings together here, under handy headings, the most frequently recurring questions and answers from his monthly feature in TODAY'S PARISH magazine.

Perennial parish council problems are extensively treated: Pastors, Members, Proper and Fair Procedure, Liturgy, Women in the Church and many others. There are also two splendid chapters on the whole theory of Church and Parish and on the relationship between different ministries. The pastoral wisdom and expertise of Fr. Rademacher are always very much in evidence.

This is the ideal quick-reference work for people in parish ministry who, faced with a new problem, don't know where to turn. $1.75

DO YOU *REALLY* KNOW THE CHURCH?
by Paul Todd — In recent years the
Church has tended to emphasize what
makes her like other religious bodies
and soft-pedal what makes her different. Plain speaking seems to have become almost a lost art.

It is time we stopped saying that we
don't know what the Church teaches.
We DO know — but are afraid to say it!
True Ecumenism calls for straight answers to straight questions. You will
find such questions — and answers — in
this informative book.

$1.75

CATHOLIC PENTECOSTALS NOW:

Ten years ago the Catholic Pentecostal Movement had its first, timid beginnings. Today it
is worldwide. Figures mentioned at the end of
1976 put the total membership as close to
three million — higher than the official calcu-
lation, but not unlikely.

Books on Charismatics abound — indeed the
Movement has its own extremely active Com-
munications' arm — but after ten years there
is need for a new study of how it looks today.
This book offers such a study and one marked
by brevity, clarity and admirable objectivity.
If you would like a succint summary of all that
has happened up to now and, more impor-
tantly, what is likely to happen over the next
decade, this book is for you.

$1.75